Non-fiction Voyage 2

Series Advisers
Shirley Bickler and Raewyn Hickey

Contents

Newspaper reports Jillian Powell
The Sensory Garden 2
Dare-U! 6

Instructions Jan Henderson
How to Defeat a Roman Army 10
How To Be a Viking 11

Information texts Jillian Powell
Woodland Habitats 12
Coastal Habitats 16

Explanations Claire Llewellyn
How Do We Move? 20
How We Move With Muscles and Bones 22

Persuasive texts Raewyn Hickey
Show Them You Care 24
The Big Paint! 26

Discussion texts Claire Llewellyn
Should Animals Be Kept In Zoos? 28
Should We Kill Animals For Food? 30

Index 32

OXFORD
UNIVERSITY PRESS

The Sensory Garden

Here you can see the articles that appeared in a local newspaper and a national newspaper when some schoolchildren developed a garden for elderly people living in a care home.

Local newspaper

Garden opens at Hillingdon House

Family and friends joined residents for the opening of the new sensory garden at Hillingdon House Care Home on Saturday.

The garden is the result of a new national project. It has been funded with the help of local businesses including Caraways Garden Centre. Year 4 children at the nearby Wood View School designed and planted a garden for residents and their families to enjoy. The school helped raise funds

Children and residents celebrate the opening of the garden

for plants by holding a strawberry tea and a three-legged walk in the summer.

The schoolchildren talked to residents and staff to find out their needs before planning the garden. Nine-year-old Jamie Chan said: "Some people use wheelchairs so we had to make sure it was easy for them. All the paths are nice and flat, and wide enough for wheelchairs to pass. The flowers and plants are in raised beds, so everyone can touch and smell them."

Wood View's headteacher, Mrs Helen O'Neill, said: "The children started by thinking about the five senses. They then used the internet and library to choose plants for each sense." Mrs O'Neill added that the children also wanted to encourage wildlife. "They wanted sounds of birdsong and bees in the garden too, so they chose plants with colour and scent."

The children had help from local garden designer Rosa Malawa. "They had some brilliant ideas, like a bubbling water fountain for sound."

Many of the children were keen to include taste. They planted herbs like mint and thyme in raised beds, so everyone could enjoy the feel and smell of them.

For many of the children, this was their first experience of gardening. Mrs O'Neill says that some of them definitely have green fingers. "They took part at every stage, right up to planting and watering the new plants," she said. "The project has also inspired class work, such as painting and drawing, and some of the children have written poems about the garden."

The children's artwork and poems are on display at Hillingdon House, along with photographs taken while the garden was being made.

Manager Peter Thorn said: "We are delighted with our new garden. It will provide a great benefit to everyone who comes to Hillingdon House."

Resident Angela Painton, agreed, saying: "It's lovely to have a beautiful place to sit with family or friends, somewhere nice and quiet with lovely smells."

Community garden scheme takes off

A sensory garden designed by school children has opened at a care home in the Midlands.

It is the first of a number of schemes around the country aiming to bring the benefits of a garden to people living in care homes and sheltered communities. Manager of Hillington House Care Home Peter Thorn said the residents were delighted. Many of the plants and features were chosen by Year 4 children from the nearby Wood View School. Headteacher Mrs Helen O'Neill said the project had given many of the children their first experience of gardening. The garden was planned with the help of designer Rosa Malawa. She said the children had come up with some inspired ideas including a herb garden and a water feature. "The children spoke to residents and staff to find out what they would like," she said. "They were very aware of issues such as access for wheelchair-users, as well as looking for plants and features that everyone could enjoy." The garden was funded by donations from local businesses and by charity events organized by the school.

The benefits of the sensory garden initiative will be felt nationwide.

Dare-U!

Here you can see the articles that appeared in a local newspaper and a national newspaper when some schoolchildren contributed to plans for a village skate park and play area.

Local newspaper

Thrills and spills as new skate park opens

State-of-the-art facilities for popular wheel sports

Burnley's new skate park and play area had its grand opening on Saturday. Local youngsters showed off their tricks on the ramps and rails, to the sounds of music from local band 'Gilded.'

Sk8 magazine's editor Jimmy Goodman and storyteller Jan Lessing were among those helping to celebrate the opening.

The skate park offers local youngsters state-of-the-art facilities for popular wheel sports including skateboarding, BMX, scooters and roller blading. There is also a play area for younger children with a colourful story wall painted by children from Burnley Middle School.

Councillor Neeta Madan said the park had been a community effort, and everyone would benefit from the new amenity. "There is a real need for this sort of thing in the village," she said. "Parents and children have been crying out for somewhere for children to play safely. We wanted to give the kids a chance to get involved right from the start, so we talked to pupils at Burnley Middle School to get their ideas of what they wanted to see."

Headteacher Mr John Holbrook said that Year 4 children had contributed ideas for the design of ramps and rails in the wheel sport area, and had also come up with their own designs for the story wall. "Some of the children are keen skateboarders, and they had some great ideas for how things could work," he said. "This project has brought design and technology to life for them. They feel it is their park, and we are confident they will enjoy it and look after it because they had a hand in creating it."

Nine-year-old Joshua Simon said: "We were always getting kicked off car parks and shopping centres by the police or security guards. Now we have somewhere where it's okay for us to practise."

Joshua's mother, Ruth Simon, agreed. "This will keep them out of trouble, and hopefully get them away from the computers to get some fresh air and exercise."

Younger children are catered for with a soft play area surrounded by a semi-circular story wall. This features colourful designs including animals, aliens and dinosaurs, painted by Year 4 children. Storyteller Jan Lessing said: "The images are great for inspiring the imagination, and engaging children in listening to and creating stories." Jan worked with a group of children from Burnley Primary to create the wall's first story, about an octopus kidnapped by aliens.

A local government initiative provided the major funding for the park. Parents and children helped with fundraising by organizing sponsored activities and competitions. The wheel sports area, named 'Dare-U!' after a children's competition to name the park, has a series of pipes, ramps and rails for the most ambitious skater.

"It was marvellous seeing our plans come to life,' Councillor Madan said. 'Some of the aerobatics performed on the bowl and ramps were amazing, and the younger children had fun exploring their own play area, which will give parents somewhere to meet and chat as well, while the children play safely."

National newspaper

Burnley's Dare-U! skate park: a community effort

Safe play initiative in Burnley

A new skate park and play area has opened in Burnley, following a two-year campaign by local residents for somewhere safe to play.

Local planners consulted with Year 4 children from Burnley Middle School to find out what they would like to see in the park, redeveloped from a run-down playground. The children contributed ideas for the design of the wheeled sports area, and took part in a project to paint a story wall for younger children. Burnley's 'Dare-U' skate park is one of a number of parks springing up around the country, to overcome the lack of facilities and meet the increasing popularity with youngsters of wheel sports such as BMX and skate-boarding. Some projects have faced opposition from residents worried about noise and nuisance, and even drugs and vandalism. But Councillor Neeta Madan is confident the new park at Burnley will benefit the whole community. "We have a lot of families in our village, and there is a real need for this sort of amenity," she said. "Involving the children in planning the project has given them an interest in maintaining and enjoying it. We're confident it will be a great success."

How to Defeat a Roman Army

By the 2nd century AD the Roman army had conquered most of the known world, but never managed to subdue the Pictish tribes of Scotland. So, how did these savage, scattered tribes defeat the overwhelming and well-trained forces of the Roman Empire?

1 Paint yourselves.

The Picts painted themselves blue and tattooed their faces to look even wilder. That's why the Romans called them Picts. It was short for Pictured People.

2 Wear little or no clothing when you attack.

This shows the Romans how tough you are, especially if it's snowing.

3 Scream a lot as you run towards them.

By this time the Romans are terrified!

4 Run away and hide.

The Romans are still too strong to beat, but they won't follow you into the trees or mountains where you can easily ambush them.

5 Start all over again.

If you repeat this enough times, the Romans will decide you are far too much bother to conquer. Especially if you follow the most important rule – number 6.

6 Live somewhere cold, wet and mountainous where crops don't grow very well.

How to Be a Viking

The Vikings lived in the Scandinavian countries between the 8th and 15th centuries. They are often seen as hairy savages with horns on their helmets who did nothing but pillage and kill. It's not entirely true. To be a real Viking you have to follow these simple instructions.

1 Treat your partner as equal.

Viking men did the raiding and trading but the women had complete say over how the household and the family estate were run. Some even took part in the battles!

2 Take care of your appearance.

Vikings wore jewellery and used combs, tweezers, toothpicks and eye makeup (including the men). They didn't wash too often, though!

3 Build cool ships.

Viking ships were better than anyone else's at the time, with different designs for trading, raiding and long distance voyages. That's how they managed to cross the Atlantic long before Christopher Columbus.

4 Be noble and courageous.

The Vikings hated thieves, but considered raids on other countries to be a test of bravery! Because they had fought for the treasures they carried off, they didn't consider it stealing. Unfortunately the people they raided didn't quite see things that way – hence their bad reputation to this day!

Woodland

Woodland Wildlife

Tree Creeper

Length: 13 centimetres
Habitat: Well-grown woodlands. April to June.
Appearance: Male and female brown with white streaks. Long curved bill.
Eggs: 5–7, white with reddish brown spots.
Food: Mainly insects and spiders.

Bluebell

Wild hyacinth. Bulb.

Height: up to 50 centimetres.
Habitat: widespread in woods and hedge banks, April to June.
Flowers: scented, usually blue-violet, sometimes white or pink, April to June.
Fruits: egg-shaped, seeds black.

Speckled Wood butterfly

Habitat: woodlands and hedgerows, late March to early October

Life cycle

Welcome to Moreton Woods

There are three routes leading from the car park.

- The Green Route is 2.5 km (about 1.5 miles) long. Allow 45 mins. The route is mostly on level paths and is suitable for prams and wheelchairs. There are sculptures along the way.
- The Yellow Route is 3 km (about 2 miles) long. Allow an hour. It includes slopes and some steps and provides occasional views over the River Carven.
- The Blue Route is 6 km (about 4 miles) long and is suitable for walkers and cyclists. It links with the Carven walkway along the river. Allow 1½–2 hours on foot.

Please follow the Forest Code when enjoying this beautiful area.

- Guard against all risk of fire.
- Protect trees, plants and wildlife.
- Leave things as you find them; take nothing away.
- Keep dogs under control.
- Avoid damaging buildings, fences, hedges, walls and signs.
- Leave no litter.

Dead Wood Lives!

Dead trees are more than just good for firewood. A piece of dead wood just 2 metres long by 50 centimetres diameter can provide a micro-habitat for up to 50 species. Fungus breaks down dead wood to provide food for insects. Wood-boring beetles lay eggs on fallen logs and their larvae feed on the decaying wood. Bees, wasps and other insects hibernate in holes and cracks. Woodland birds such as nuthatches and tree creepers feed on insects by pecking into cracks and crevices.

Go tracking! Look out for these woodland animal tracks.

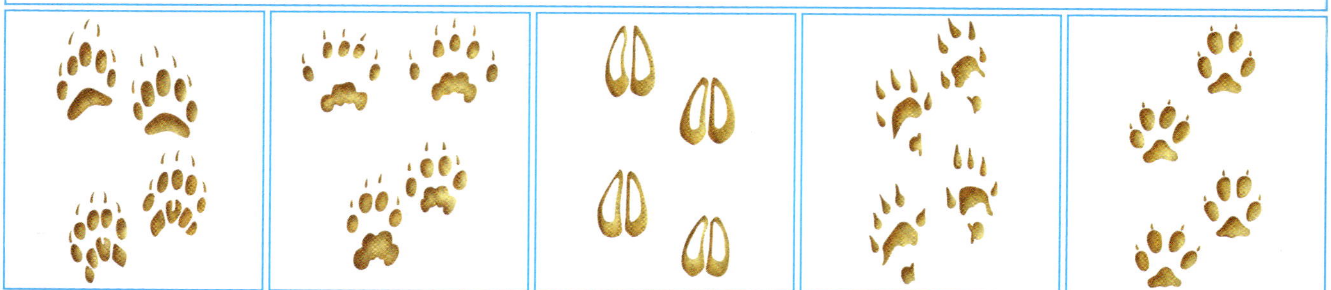

badger	squirrel	fallow deer	stoat	fox

Standish Wood O.S. SO 80 (832086) 3.2 km

From the farm gate, take the path on the right, marked by a yellow arrow and white dot. The path winds down between some fine beeches. In spring, the ground is carpeted with bluebells and primroses. In autumn, look out for fungi growing on the leaf litter or on dead woods and stumps.

The path widens between younger beech and ash trees and some shrubby undergrowth. Look out for grey squirrels and badger setts as you go. In summer, this is a good place to see the Speckled Wood butterfly. Standish Wood is particularly known for its woodland butterflies and moths.

Woodland Management Volunteer Day

Brandon Wood, near Coventry
Saturday 5th April, 9.30–5.00

Meet at Visitor centre, 9 a.m.

What to bring

- Suitable outdoor clothes
- Stout boots or wellies
- Waterproofs
- Sandwiches
- Enthusiasm!

Back Forward Stop Refresh Home AutoFill Print Mail

Address: http://badger-intro/watching...

Badger Watching

The best time for badger watching is on spring evenings, when the cubs are active.

Badgers will quickly pick up your scent so stand where the wind is blowing away from the sett. Use trees, bushes or a hide for camouflage, and wear dark clothing.

Be patient and keep very quiet while waiting for badgers to come out of a sett. You may hear them foraging for food before you see them. Use a red filter torch, which should not disturb the badgers, but avoid flash photography.

Go to http://badger-intro/watching...

Coastal Habitats

Constantine Bay

The beach at Constantine Bay is sheltered by low headlands and rocky islands. There are large sand dunes to the rear of the beach. These have been planted with marram grass to help stabilize them.

The beach provides many rock pools which are well worth exploring. The coastal path traces the curve of the bay over the low cliffs and has spectacular sea views.

- *Life Guard*
- *Seasonal Tidy Britain Group Award*
- *Swim*
- *Surf*
- *Shop 400 m up the road*

parking P toilets accessible toilets visitor information i no dogs

TAKE PARTICULAR NOTE OF THE SAFETY NOTICES.

Back Forward Stop Refresh Home AutoFill Print Mail

Address: http://surfing-world/...

search Go

UK Surfing Tomorrow

Observed at Thursday 7 a.m.

	Location	Wave Height (cm)	Wind
1.	Aberdeen	60	SW2 Decreasing
2.	Bournem'h	none	N1 No change
3.	Cayton	none	W4 Decreasing
4.	Croyde	30	W3 Similar
5.	Gower	0–30	NW2 Similar
6.	Hebrides	120	W5 Increasing
7.	Hells M'h	none	W2 Similar
8.	Newquay	30	NW3 Similar

Go to http://surfing-world/...

Coastal Erosion

The coastline is constantly wearing away. The wind and the tide can erode soft cliffs, low-lying land, sand dunes and salt marshes. People can cause erosion along paths and fragile areas such as soft sand dunes. Coastal plants that are trampled by feet or vehicles can die out, leaving bare ground which is then eroded by weather. Erosion and disturbance cause habitats to change and many sensitive plant and animal species begin to disappear.

How you can help:

- Respect the coastal environment.
- Don't leave litter on beaches.
- Don't trample on plants.
- Don't pick wildflowers or disturb wildlife.
- Don't dig into soft sand dunes.
- Avoid walking on fragile areas which are signed or roped off.

Kittiwake

Length: 38 – 43 cm.

Smaller and slimmer than common gull. Grey upper parts, white under parts, wings pointed, black triangle at tip. Feeds from sea surface in flight. Skilful diver for fish and marine invertebrates. Breeds on sea cliffs, port buildings and piers. Nests on cliff ledges. 1–3 eggs, late May – mid August. Noisy when nesting, with cries of 'Kitti-week.'

Coastal Collection : Card 12

Marram grass

Perennial. Grows only on sandy coasts. Common on sand dunes. Stout, upright stem, 60–120 cm tall. Creeping root which binds the sand around its base. Long, stiff pointed leaves, rolled inwards, smooth on the outside, rough inside, bluish-green in colour. Spike-like flower head. Flowers June to August. The caterpillar of the shore wainscot moth feeds on it from August to May.

COASTAL PLANTS 12

13 Identification Guide

Seal Trips

Boat trips to see the birds and seals. Landing on Blakeney Point. Trips last 1–2 hours, depending on the tides. At the far point of the creek you can see seals in their natural habitat. The colony numbers about 500 grey seals. Bring cameras as the boats are able to get close to the basking seals.

Tickets
Adults: £14 Children under 14: £4

Grey Seal Facts

Britain's largest wild mammal.

Weight: Males weigh around 275 kg, females 180 kg.

Life span: males 35 years, females 20 years.

Food: around 5 kg a day of fish, sand eels, molluscs and crustaceans.

Speed: Swim at 12 miles per hour, can dive up to 60 metres.

Young: Pups born in the autumn.

Where to see them: coasts of North Norfolk, Northumbria, Cornwall, Devon, Pembrokeshire and Ceredigion, and around the Farne Islands.

Coastal walk

From the Perranporth Youth Hostel follow the cliff path. You will get spectacular views from Cligga Head. The path drops down to a cove where you will find a surfing beach. Walking up from the cove towards St Agnes Head, look out for nesting kittiwakes, guillemots and razorbills. The path passes through St Agnes, which has many old miners' cottages and a museum in an old chapel. From St Agnes Head, on a clear day, you can see shearwater, terns and many of the more common gulls.

How Do We Move?

Every time we move we use our muscles. Many of our muscles are joined to bones. When the muscles pull on the bones, our body moves.

Bones and joints

Our body contains over 200 bones. These bones meet at places called joints. For example, in our arm we have three joints – at the shoulder, elbow and wrist. These are the places where our arm can move when our muscles pull on the bones.

How muscles work

Muscles are made of long, stringy fibres. These fibres grow shorter or longer when they get messages from the brain. If the fibres get shorter, they pull on a bone. If the fibres grow longer, they stop pulling. Muscles can pull but they cannot push. Because of this, many muscles work in pairs: one muscle pulls a bone up, the other pulls it back again.

This **muscle** pulls on the bone in the lower arm to make the arm straighten.

The weightlifter wants to lift the weight up to his chest.

Bending the arm

The muscles in our upper arm work as a pair. We use one muscle to bend the arm. To straighten it, we use the other.

Now the other muscle straightens the arm to lift the weight.

How We Move With Muscles and Bones

Sitting, standing, bending, jumping – our every movement depends on muscles and bones. When muscles contract, they pull on the bones and our body begins to move.

Muscle power

Muscles are made of bundles of fibres, each one thinner than a hair. The fibres can contract or relax when the brain instructs them to do so. When they contract, the muscle grows shorter and pulls on a bone. When they relax, the muscle grows longer and stops pulling on the bone. Muscles cannot push; they can only pull. Because of this, many muscles work in pairs to pull bones from opposite directions.

Bones, joints and tendons

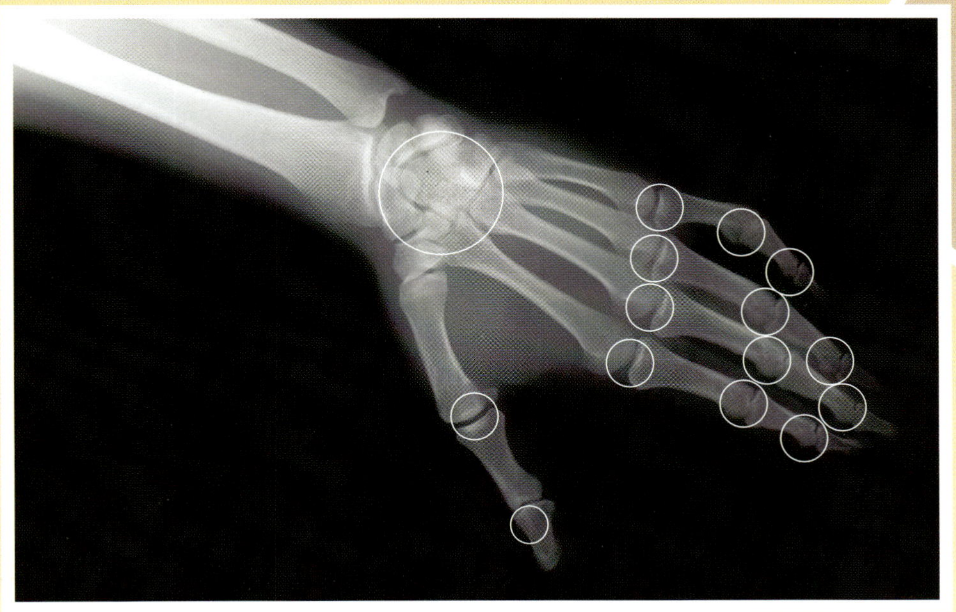

Joints in our fingers and wrist allow our hands to move in many different ways.

Our skeleton contains over 200 bones. The bones are joined at places called joints, such as the shoulder, knuckle or knee. These are the points where our bones can move. Muscles are attached to the bones by tough cords called tendons.

Bending the arm

The biceps and triceps muscles work together to move the arm.

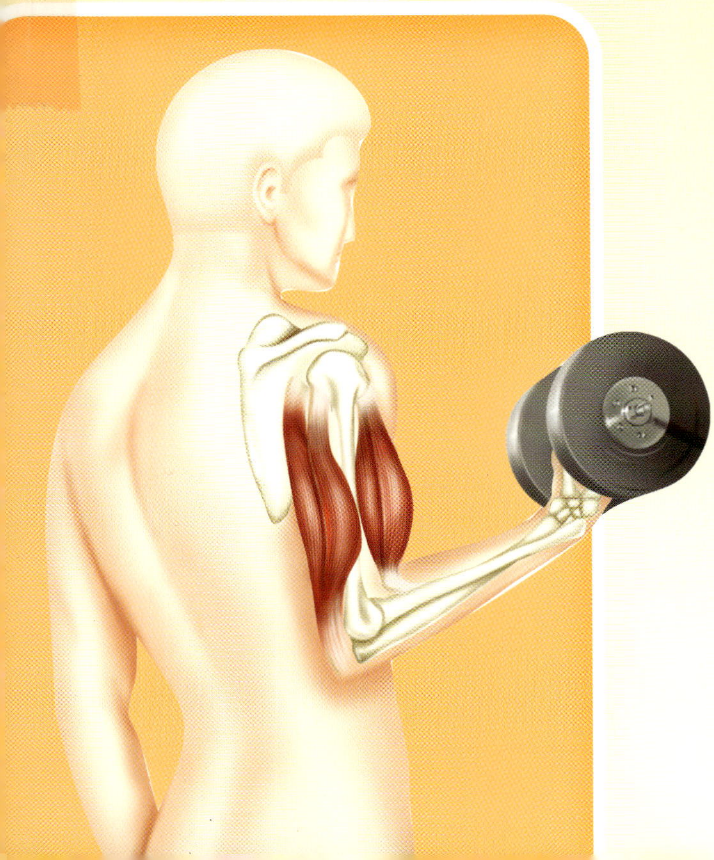

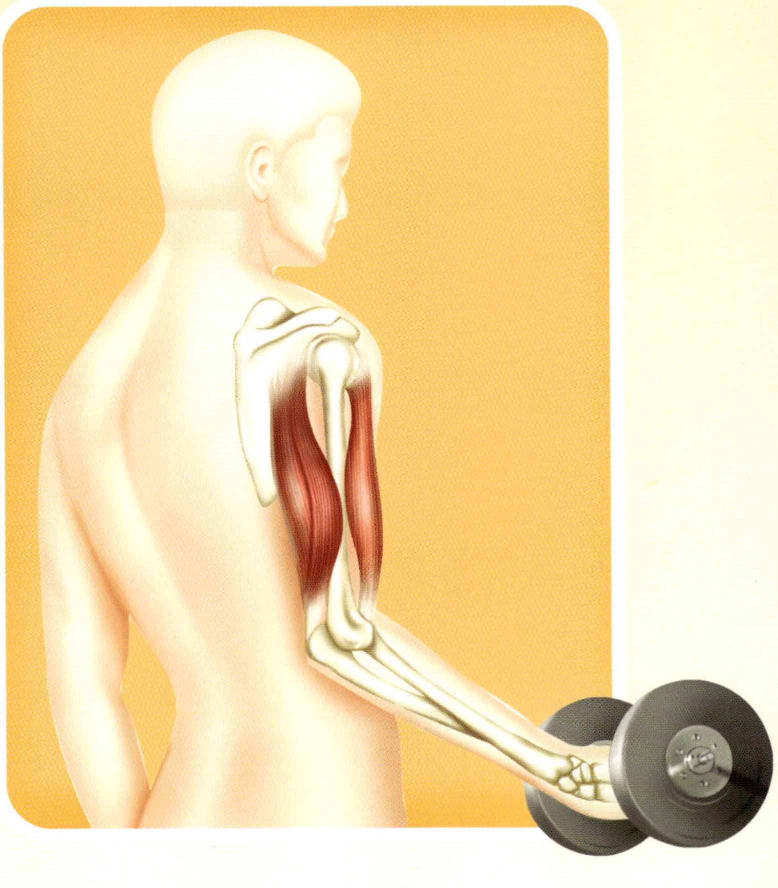

Show Them You Care

Support the Mayor's Trust Fund for Children

Join in

The Big Paint!

Saturday 3rd March, 10–4 Newstead Shopping Centre

Help others while you have fun!

The Mayor's Trust Fund for Children invites you to create an eye-catching T-shirt that everyone will want!

What? A unique event where you can design your own T-shirt and help others. You get something great to wear, and The Mayor's Trust Fund for Children gets the money it so desperately needs to make children's lives better.

Why? The MTFFC supports children's charities, providing fun and facilities where they're most needed. With YOUR help we can do so much more!

How? All you have to do is paint a picture for a T-shirt. It's that easy! Our experts will be on hand if you need any inspiration, and your design will be printed on a T-shirt, ready for you to buy, in just 30 minutes!

Who? Absolutely everyone! The more we paint, the more we raise!

Every T-shirt sold enables the MTFFC to enrich more children's lives. Look how your T-shirt can help:

Profits from T-shirts	What we could buy
5 T-shirts	A football
10 T-shirts	A cinema trip for a family in care
25 T-shirts	Three teddy bears
50 T-shirts	A toddler's trike
100 T-shirts	A cot and mattress
200 T-shirts	A weekend away for a sick child

Enjoy Being Generous

Why not buy or design more than one T-shirt for a really individual present for friends and family?

Remember, every T-shirt you buy will help the MTFFC to help more children.

The Big Paint!

Be Creative! Get Crafty!

Have Fun!

Open Workshop
Saturday 3 March, 10–4
Newstead Shopping Centre

Come along and join the fun at Newstead Shopping Centre. Create an eye-catching design and have it printed on your very own T-shirt!

It's so easy. You design your picture and the rest will be done for you. Your T-shirt will be printed and ready for you to buy in just 30 minutes! All money raised goes to the Mayor's Trust Fund for Children, giving a helping hand to children's charities.

Delight your family!

This is so much fun, you'll want to design more than one. Choose any size T-shirt and design a really special gift.

Be a winner!

The best design of the day will be printed and sold in children's fashion store *Puff'n'Stuff,* in aid of the Mayor's Trust Fund for Children.

Meet the experts and learn some new techniques!

Have a great day out supporting the MTFFC!

Should animals be kept in zoos?

Many people feel strongly about zoos. Some people think that zoos can help animals. Others think that zoos are cruel, and should be closed down. What are the arguments on each side?

Some animals, such as pandas and tigers, are getting very rare. They are in danger of extinction. If these animals are kept in zoos, they can be protected. Scientists can study them and help them to breed. In time, they can be returned to the wild.

Life in the zoo: playground . . . or prison?

But how often does this happen? Up to five million animals are kept in zoos around the world, and very few of them are ever returned to the wild. What's more, many zoo animals are not in danger of extinction. For monkeys, seals, giraffes and bears, zoos are a jail for life.

However, zoos are clearly safe places. They give the animals food and water, and care for them when they are ill. A wolf cub will not starve in winter; a young zebra is free from attack. On the other hand, what kind of life do these animals have? The world's best zoos look after their animals, but the worst ones keep them in small cages and bare concrete yards. It's no wonder that the gorillas look sad and the lions pace up and down in such places.

Many people are interested in animals but cannot travel around the world to see them in their natural habitats. In zoos they can watch penguins swimming and hear a real lion roar. This is better than looking at books or watching pictures on a screen. In addition, a zoo is like a living classroom. Some children enjoy the animals so much that they want to become scientists.

However, many people just make faces at the animals and then hurry to the shop. They learn nothing from zoos. Perhaps this is because zoos are not natural. Films about animals in the wild can teach us so much more.

So are zoos good or bad? What do you think? Which side are you on?

Should We Kill Animals For Food?

For many years people have argued about whether it is right to kill animals for food. Vegetarians believe that eating animals is wrong while meat-eaters strongly disagree.

Some animals have freedom to roam on farms.

Vegetarians argue that animals are intelligent. They can feel the same fear and pain as humans, so how can it be right to kill them? On the other hand, meat-eaters argue that humans have killed and eaten animals for a long time, and that it is part of our nature. In addition to this, meat is an important part of our diet. It is not only tasty but also a quick and easy way to get the protein we need in order to be healthy. It is much harder to get protein from a meat-free diet. Vegetarians strongly disagree. They argue that far from being necessary for our survival, meat has caused a huge rise in heart disease, cancer and other serious illnesses.

Farming is another matter for debate. Vegetarians and vegans condemn modern factory farms, where chickens are kept in such small cages that they cannot flap their wings, and cows are pumped full of chemicals and given the wrong kind of food. Some say that such farms might infect us with food poisoning and mad cows' disease. Many meat-eaters actually agree with this view. They prefer free-range farms, where animals are given a decent life and a humane death.

Some animals have less freedom.

Animal farming has hidden benefits. Many of us enjoy the countryside, with its rolling fields, hedges and dry stone walls. This landscape was created by animal farmers. Without them, meat-eaters argue, it would begin to disappear. Vegetarians protest that arable farmers are just as able to care for the countryside and that growing food crops rather than raising farm animals is a much better use of the land. In fact, by growing crops on land now used for grazing, we could produce enough food to end world famine.

So is it right to eat animals or not? There are strong arguments and feelings on both sides of the question. Everyone has their own point of view. What's yours?

Index

badger 15
biceps 23
birds,
- kittiwake 18
- nuthatch 14
- tree creeper 12

bones 20-23
butterfly,
speckled wood 12, 14
care home 2-5
conservation 12-19, 28-29
countryside 12-19, 30-31
erosion 17
extinction 28
farming 30-31
food 30-31
Forest Code 13
fund-raising 2, 8, 24-27
garden 2-5
habitat,
- coastal 16-19
- woodland 12-15

joints 20-23
meat 30-31
muscles 20-23
newspapers 2-9
painting 24-27
Picts 10
plants,
- coastal plants 19
- garden plants 2-5
- woodland plants 12

Romans 10
Scandinavia 11
seals 19
ships 11
skate park 6-9
story wall 6-9
surfing 16
triceps 23
T-shirts 24-27
vegetarians 30-31
Vikings 11
volunteering 15
walks 12-13, 19
wood 14
zoos 28-29